Make Self-Care A Priority

Your Needs Matter Too!

An inspirational journal to
cultivate healthy habits and manage stress

Gwendolyn A. Martin, Ed.D., LPC

This journal is dedicated to all who seek to make
SELF-CARE a priority!

Also by Dr. Gwen

A to Z Self-Care Guide for Educators

Self-Care Journal

This Journal belongs to

_____

The journey began on

_____

All Rights Reserved

No part of this book may be reproduced or used in any form or manner without written permission of the copyright owner except for the use of quotations in a book review.

Copyright © 2021 by Gwendolyn A. Martin

ISBN: 978-1-7364413-1-2

My Message to YOU

Self-care is a process. It begins with self-awareness and prioritizing the value of you as a person. Self-care is an important tool to help you live a more abundant life. Our day-to-day lives are usually filled with endless responsibilities. It is often hard to find solitude and take time to practice self-care in today's climate. Many of us are feeling the stresses of the present state of our world and economy. The seemingly constant cycle of negative news does not make matters any easier. It is crucial that you make self-care a priority for your physical, psychological, emotional, spiritual, and professional health and well-being at this very moment. Self-care can come in the form of simply stepping out into nature, reading an inspiring book, or indulging in your favorite hobby to ensure that you are taking the time you need for yourself. Incorporating small daily activities into everyday routines can make you healthier and happier.

Right NOW, self-care is more important than ever. Do not feel guilty if you need to take some time for yourself, even if it is taking a long hot bath or adhering to boundaries you have set for family, friends, and colleagues. This journal is designed to help you develop self-empathy and self-compassion: the capacity to notice, value and respond to your own needs as generously as you attend to the needs of others. Throughout this journal, I shared some of my favorite self-care quotes to jump-start positive thinking and highlight the importance of taking necessary YOU time. Remember your needs matter too! Today is the beginning of your journey to better health and wellness. Start taking time to do things that make you happy and make you feel fulfilled, loved, and appreciated. Every day is a new growth opportunity. I cannot wait to hear how far you go and how much you grow.

HOW TO GET THE BEST RESULTS OUT OF YOUR SELF-CARE JOURNEY

There is no need to go to India or anywhere else to find peace. You will find that deep place of silence right in your room, your garden or even your bathtub.
~ *Elisabeth Kubler-Ross*

How Your Self-Care Journal Works
Each day of writing begins with an expression of gratitude for things big and small that you have, are thankful for, and do not take for granted.
It is followed by:
- Self-care strategies and tools, you applied during the day to keep you balanced physically, psychologically, emotionally, spiritually, and professionally.
- Affirming your progress through three positive *I am* statements. These positive affirmations statements will help you confront and control negative, self-sabotaging thoughts and make positive changes.
- Writing goals and self-care strategies for the next day to keep you accountable and on track to better health and wellness.
- Evaluating how well you accomplished the daily goal you set for yourself.

PROGRESS OVER PERFECTION
We are all work in progress on this journey to better health and wellness.
- It is okay if you miss a day or two of writing in your journal.
- Do not agonize, pick back up where you left off and keep going.
- It may be helpful to set aside a designated time (10-15 minutes) to write in your journal daily. I find that right before bed works best for me.
- Always remember to do what works best for you.
- Write about whatever comes to the surface mentally or emotionally.

This is your time to reflect, release, recharge and renew. Journaling will open the door to endless growth opportunities.

COMMITMENT

How far you go and how much you grow on this self-care journey is dependent upon your level of commitment. You can achieve this by:
- Cultivating daily habits to ensure that you make self-care a priority.
- Scheduling time to reflect on each milestone.
- Celebrating your wins daily.
- Acknowledging challenges along the way.

Through commitment you gain renewed strength to keep going and growing.

RECOMMENDATIONS

I recommend you read *Dr. Gwen's A to Z Self-Care Guide* and incorporate strategies that are meaningful to you as you embark on this self-care journey. The guide contains practical solutions and self-care tips that can be easily incorporated in your existing daily routine and will inspire you to act NOW. Practice the tips, tools, and strategies in the guide and share them with your family, friends, colleagues, and community.

Let us support each other on this self-care journey to better health and wellness.

The journey begins. You Got This!

Peace and Blessings,

Dr. Gwen

SELF

Change your mindset and attitude.

Ask for help when needed.

Rest, release, recharge, and renew.

Eat healthy and exercise regularly.

Self-care is how you take your **POWER** back.

~ Lalah Delia

Self-Care Vision Board

WHAT IF YOUR VISION BOARD CAME TRUE?
YOU ARE WHAT YOU MANIFEST!

Visualization is a way to manifest your goals and dreams. Goal setting is important at every age and stage in your life. Creating a vision board can help you layout your ideal future using images (draw, cut, and paste), words (affirmations, quotes, phrases, slogans, graffiti), and emotions (joy, relief, peace).

Vision boards allow you to stop, think, and plan where you want to BE in life physically, psychologically, emotionally, spiritually, and professionally. Visuals help to make your goals and dreams more tangible and concrete.

Visual imagery will increase your motivation and determination while serving as a reminder of the life you dream of living. However, a vision board is only as beneficial as the work you are willing to put into it, so be creative and let your imagination run free as you make your vision board as thorough, exciting, and detailed as possible. Dream BIG!

THE BENEFITS

One of the most powerful benefits of creating your vision board is building confidence, solidifying your dreams, and turning thoughts into possibilities.

No matter what you believe about yourself, how much fear and self-doubt you have, a vision board completed with fidelity will slowly begin to transform self-defeating thoughts, behaviors, and beliefs. The outcome of a vision board is a more confident, self-motivated YOU!

Cultivating a growth mindset vs. a fixed mindset by:

- Clarify and fine-tune your goals as you go and grow.
- Understand that it is okay to begin with vague self-care goals.
- Remember progress over perfection is the goal; the important thing is that you START.

MY TOP 5 TIPS TO CREATING YOUR SELF-CARE VISION BOARD:

1. **Schedule Time to Create It** – Take time to focus on yourself. Light a candle, turn on some feel-good music, and let the visualization begin. This should be a fun time spent getting in touch with your innermost thoughts, hopes, and dreams.

2. **Ask: What Makes YOU Most Happy?** – "Happy" means something different to everybody. Think of the people, places, and things that make you happiest and find ways to incorporate more of that positive energy into your life.

3. **Find Visual Representations** – Find images and words (in magazines or online) that relate to the dreams and goals you expressed above. Use images that offer you the best visual of your desired results.

4. **Make a Collage** – Use the space provided on the next page to draw (art, doodle, symbols, stick figures) or paste various items such as photographs, quotes, affirmations, magazine clippings etc., to depict your ideal future. Be creative, have fun, and remember it is okay to think outside the box and color outside the lines.

5. **Look at it and update often** – Visualize living your dream life right NOW. Every time you look at your vision board, you will be reminded of your goals and dreams. Remember, our lives are continually changing, so you should check images and goals off the board as they are accomplished and add new ones in their place.

MY FAVORITE IDEAS TO HELP YOU GET STARTED

Supply List
Crayons/Colored Pencils or Pens
Markers or Sharpies
Pencils
Glue
Magazines
Scissors
Scrapbook paper

Have Fun!

Categories
Body & Health
Bucket List
Career & Life Path
Family
Finances
Friendships & Sociability
Hobbies
Love & Relationships
Skills/Learning
Travel
World & Community

Items to Consider
Affirmations
Brochures
Cards (post, business, personal)
Famous Quotes
Maps
People You Admire
Pictures
Scrapbook Paper
Stickers
Tickets

Create YOUR Vision Board

It is important to take time for yourself and find clarity. The most important relationship is the one you have with yourself.

~ Diane Von Furstenberg

Self-Care Affirmations

I am beautiful inside and out.

I am attracting positive people and experiences in my life.

I am open to new opportunities.

JOURNAL ENTRY

Day: _____ Date: _____/_____/_____

Today I am grateful for _____

_____

_____

_____

I practiced self-care today by _____

_____

_____

_____

_____

_____

_____

_____

_____

_____

_____

♡ ♡ ♡ ♡ Daily Affirmations ♡ ♡ ♡ ♡

I am _____

I am _____

I am _____

Plan Your Work and Work Your Plan!

Set Goal _____

_____

_____

Plan Strategy _____

_____

_____

Outcome _____

_____

_____

Day: _____ Date: _____ / _____ / _____

Today I am grateful for _____

_____

_____

_____

I practiced self-care today by_____

_____

_____

_____

_____

_____

_____

_____

_____

_____

♡ ♡ ♡ ♡ Daily Affirmations ♡ ♡ ♡ ♡

I am _____

I am _____

I am _____

> Plan Your Work and Work Your Plan!

Set Goal _____
_____
_____

Plan Strategy _____
_____
_____

Outcome _____
_____
_____

Day: _____ Date: _____/ _____/ _____ ♥

Today I am grateful for _____

_____

_____

_____

I practiced self-care today by_____

_____

_____

_____

_____

_____

_____

_____

_____

_____

_____

♡ ♡ ♡ ♡ Daily Affirmations ♡ ♡ ♡ ♡

I am _____

I am _____

I am _____

> Plan Your Work and Work Your Plan!

Set Goal _____

_____

_____

Plan Strategy _____

_____

_____

Outcome _____

_____

_____

Day: _____ Date: _____/_____/_____

Today I am grateful for _____

_____

_____

_____

I practiced self-care today by_____

_____

_____

_____

_____

_____

_____

_____

_____

_____

_____

♡ ♡ ♡ ♡ Daily Affirmations ♡ ♡ ♡ ♡

I am _____

I am _____

I am _____

Plan Your Work and Work Your Plan!

Set Goal _____

_____

_____

Plan Strategy _____

_____

_____

Outcome _____

_____

_____

Day: _____ Date: _____/ _____/ _____

Today I am grateful for _____

_____

_____

_____

I practiced self-care today by_____

_____

_____

_____

_____

_____

_____

_____

_____

_____

_____

♡ ♡ ♡ ♡ Daily Affirmations ♡ ♡ ♡ ♡

I am _____

I am _____

I am _____

> Plan Your Work and Work Your Plan!

Set Goal _____

_____

_____

Plan Strategy _____

_____

_____

Outcome _____

_____

_____

Day: _____ Date: _____/_____/_____

Today I am grateful for _____

_____

_____

_____

I practiced self-care today by_____

_____

_____

_____

_____

_____

_____

_____

_____

_____

_____

_____

♡ ♡ ♡ ♡ Daily Affirmations ♡ ♡ ♡ ♡

I am _____

I am _____

I am _____

Plan Your Work and Work Your Plan!

Set Goal _____

_____

_____

Plan Strategy _____

_____

_____

Outcome _____

_____

_____

Day: _____ Date: _____/_____/_____

Today I am grateful for _____

_____

_____

_____

I practiced self-care today by_____

_____

_____

_____

_____

_____

_____

_____

_____

_____

_____

♡ ♡ ♡ ♡ Daily Affirmations ♡ ♡ ♡ ♡

I am _____

I am _____

I am _____

Plan Your Work and Work Your Plan!

Set Goal _____

_____

_____

Plan Strategy _____

_____

_____

Outcome _____

_____

_____

Reflect, Release, Recharge & Renew
♡ Positive Self-Talk ONLY ♡
Talk to yourself like you would someone you LOVE. ~ Brené Brown

It's not selfish to love yourself, take care of yourself, and make your happiness a priority. It's necessary.

~ Mandy Hale

Self-Care Affirmations

I am in the process of becoming the best version of myself.

I am on the right path. I am moving in the right direction.

I am determined to be healthy and happy.

Day: _____ Date: _____/_____/_____ ♥

Today I am grateful for _____

_____

_____

_____

I practiced self-care today by_____

_____

_____

_____

_____

_____

_____

_____

_____

_____

_____

♡ ♡ ♡ ♡ Daily Affirmations ♡ ♡ ♡ ♡

I am _____

I am _____

I am _____

Plan Your Work and Work Your Plan!

Set Goal _____
_____
_____

Plan Strategy _____
_____
_____

Outcome _____
_____
_____

Day: _____ Date: _____/ _____/ _____

Today I am grateful for _____

_____

_____

_____

I practiced self-care today by_____

_____

_____

_____

_____

_____

_____

_____

_____

_____

_____

♡ ♡ ♡ ♡ Daily Affirmations ♡ ♡ ♡ ♡

I am _____

I am _____

I am _____

Plan Your Work and Work Your Plan!

Set Goal _____

_____

_____

Plan Strategy _____

_____

_____

Outcome _____

_____

_____

Day: _____ Date: _____/_____/_____

Today I am grateful for _____

_____

_____

_____

I practiced self-care today by_____

_____

_____

_____

_____

_____

_____

_____

_____

_____

_____

♡ ♡ ♡ ♡ Daily Affirmations ♡ ♡ ♡ ♡

I am _____

I am _____

I am _____

> Plan Your Work and Work Your Plan!

Set Goal _____
_____
_____

Plan Strategy _____
_____
_____

Outcome _____
_____
_____

Day: _____ Date: _____/_____/_____

Today I am grateful for _____
_____
_____
_____

I practiced self-care today by_____
_____
_____
_____
_____
_____
_____
_____
_____
_____
_____

♡ ♡ ♡ ♡ Daily Affirmations ♡ ♡ ♡ ♡

I am _____

I am _____

I am _____

Plan Your Work and Work Your Plan!

Set Goal _____

_____

_____

Plan Strategy _____

_____

_____

Outcome _____

_____

_____

Day: _____ Date: _____/_____/_____

Today I am grateful for _____

_____

_____

_____

I practiced self-care today by_____

_____

_____

_____

_____

_____

_____

_____

_____

_____

_____

_____

♡ ♡ ♡ ♡ Daily Affirmations ♡ ♡ ♡ ♡

I am _____

I am _____

I am _____

Plan Your Work and Work Your Plan!

Set Goal _____

_____

_____

Plan Strategy _____

_____

_____

Outcome _____

_____

_____

Day: _____ Date: _____/_____/_____ ♥

Today I am grateful for _____

_____

_____

_____

I practiced self-care today by_____

_____

_____

_____

_____

_____

_____

_____

_____

_____

_____

♡ ♡ ♡ ♡ Daily Affirmations ♡ ♡ ♡ ♡

I am _____

I am _____

I am _____

Plan Your Work and Work Your Plan!

Set Goal _____

_____

_____

Plan Strategy _____

_____

_____

Outcome _____

_____

_____

Day: _____ Date: _____/_____/_____

Today I am grateful for _____
_____
_____
_____

I practiced self-care today by_____
_____
_____
_____
_____
_____
_____
_____
_____
_____
_____
_____
_____

♡ ♡ ♡ ♡ Daily Affirmations ♡ ♡ ♡ ♡

I am _____

I am _____

I am _____

Plan Your Work and Work Your Plan!

Set Goal _____

_____

_____

Plan Strategy _____

_____

_____

Outcome _____

_____

_____

Reflect, Release, Recharge & Renew

Talk to yourself like you would someone you LOVE. ~ Brené Brown

If you feel "BURNOUT" setting in, demoralized and exhausted, it is best, for the sake of everyone, to withdraw, and RESTORE yourself.

~ Dalai Lama

Self-Care Affirmations

I am healing from the inside out.

I am taking time to rest and recharge.

I am a survivor.

Day: _____ Date: _____/ _____/ _____

Today I am grateful for _____

_____

_____

_____

I practiced self-care today by _____

_____

_____

_____

_____

_____

_____

_____

_____

_____

_____

♡ ♡ ♡ ♡ Daily Affirmations ♡ ♡ ♡ ♡

I am _____

I am _____

I am _____

Plan Your Work and Work Your Plan!

Set Goal _____

_____

_____

Plan Strategy _____

_____

_____

Outcome _____

_____

_____

Day: _____ Date: _____/_____/_____

Today I am grateful for _____

_____

_____

_____

I practiced self-care today by_____

_____

_____

_____

_____

_____

_____

_____

_____

_____

_____

_____

♡ ♡ ♡ ♡ Daily Affirmations ♡ ♡ ♡ ♡

I am _____

I am _____

I am _____

Plan Your Work and Work Your Plan!

Set Goal _____

_____

_____

Plan Strategy _____

_____

_____

Outcome _____

_____

_____

Day: _____ Date: _____/_____/_____

Today I am grateful for _____

_____

_____

_____

I practiced self-care today by_____

_____

_____

_____

_____

_____

_____

_____

_____

_____

_____

♡ ♡ ♡ ♡ Daily Affirmations ♡ ♡ ♡ ♡

I am _____

I am _____

I am _____

Plan Your Work and Work Your Plan!

Set Goal _____

_____

_____

Plan Strategy _____

_____

_____

Outcome _____

_____

_____

Day: _____ Date: _____/_____/_____

Today I am grateful for _____

_____

_____

_____

I practiced self-care today by_____

_____

_____

_____

_____

_____

_____

_____

_____

_____

_____

♡ ♡ ♡ ♡ **Daily Affirmations** ♡ ♡ ♡ ♡

I am _____

I am _____

I am _____

> Plan Your Work and Work Your Plan!

Set Goal _____

_____

_____

Plan Strategy _____

_____

_____

Outcome _____

_____

_____

Day: _____ Date: _____/_____/_____

Today I am grateful for _____

_____

_____

_____

I practiced self-care today by _____

_____

_____

_____

_____

_____

_____

_____

_____

_____

_____

♡ ♡ ♡ ♡ Daily Affirmations ♡ ♡ ♡ ♡

I am _____

I am _____

I am _____

Plan Your Work and Work Your Plan!

Set Goal _____

_____

_____

Plan Strategy _____

_____

_____

Outcome _____

_____

_____

Day: _____ Date: _____/_____/_____

Today I am grateful for _____

_____

_____

_____

I practiced self-care today by_____

_____

_____

_____

_____

_____

_____

_____

_____

_____

_____

♡ ♡ ♡ ♡ Daily Affirmations ♡ ♡ ♡ ♡

I am _____

I am _____

I am _____

Plan Your Work and Work Your Plan!

Set Goal _____
_____
_____

Plan Strategy _____
_____
_____

Outcome _____
_____
_____

Day: _____ Date: _____/ _____/ _____

Today I am grateful for _____

_____

_____

_____

I practiced self-care today by_____

_____

_____

_____

_____

_____

_____

_____

_____

_____

_____

_____

♡ ♡ ♡ ♡ Daily Affirmations ♡ ♡ ♡ ♡

I am _____

I am _____

I am _____

Plan Your Work and Work Your Plan!

Set Goal _____

_____

_____

Plan Strategy _____

_____

_____

Outcome _____

_____

_____

Reflect, Release, Recharge & Renew
♡ Positive Self-Talk ONLY ♡
Talk to yourself like you would someone you LOVE. ~ Brené Brown

When you say "YES" to others make sure you are not saying NO to yourself.

~ Paolo Coehlo

Self-Care Affirmations

I am releasing fear and doubt.

I am allowed to say "No".

I am doing things that make me feel happy and fulfilled.

Day: _____ Date: _____/ _____/ _____

Today I am grateful for _____
_____
_____
_____

I practiced self-care today by_____
_____
_____
_____
_____
_____
_____
_____
_____
_____
_____
_____

♡ ♡ ♡ ♡ Daily Affirmations ♡ ♡ ♡ ♡

I am _____

I am _____

I am _____

Plan Your Work and Work Your Plan!

Set Goal _____

_____

_____

Plan Strategy _____

_____

_____

Outcome _____

_____

_____

Day: _____ Date: _____/_____/_____   ♥

Today I am grateful for _____

_____

_____

_____

I practiced self-care today by_____

_____

_____

_____

_____

_____

_____

_____

_____

_____

_____

♡ ♡ ♡ ♡ Daily Affirmations ♡ ♡ ♡ ♡

I am _____

I am _____

I am _____

Plan Your Work and Work Your Plan!

Set Goal _____

_____

_____

Plan Strategy _____

_____

_____

Outcome _____

_____

_____

Day: _____ Date: _____/ _____/ _____

Today I am grateful for _____

_____

_____

_____

I practiced self-care today by_____

_____

_____

_____

_____

_____

_____

_____

_____

_____

_____

♡ ♡ ♡ ♡ Daily Affirmations ♡ ♡ ♡ ♡

I am _____

I am _____

I am _____

Plan Your Work and Work Your Plan!

Set Goal _____

_____

_____

Plan Strategy _____

_____

_____

Outcome _____

_____

_____

Day: _____ Date: _____/_____/_____

Today I am grateful for _____

_____

_____

_____

I practiced self-care today by_____

_____

_____

_____

_____

_____

_____

_____

_____

_____

_____

♡ ♡ ♡ ♡ Daily Affirmations ♡ ♡ ♡ ♡

I am _____

I am _____

I am _____

Plan Your Work and Work Your Plan!

Set Goal _____
_____
_____

Plan Strategy _____
_____
_____

Outcome _____
_____
_____

Day: _____ Date: _____/_____/_____   ♥

Today I am grateful for _____

_____

_____

_____

I practiced self-care today by_____

_____

_____

_____

_____

_____

_____

_____

_____

_____

_____

♡ ♡ ♡ ♡ Daily Affirmations ♡ ♡ ♡ ♡

I am _____

I am _____

I am _____

Plan Your Work and Work Your Plan!

Set Goal _____

_____

_____

Plan Strategy _____

_____

_____

Outcome _____

_____

_____

Day: _____ Date: _____/_____/_____

Today I am grateful for _____

_____

_____

_____

I practiced self-care today by_____

_____

_____

_____

_____

_____

_____

_____

_____

_____

_____

♡ ♡ ♡ ♡ Daily Affirmations ♡ ♡ ♡ ♡

I am _____

I am _____

I am _____

Plan Your Work and Work Your Plan!

Set Goal _____
_____
_____

Plan Strategy _____
_____
_____

Outcome _____
_____
_____

Day: _____ Date: _____/_____/_____

Today I am grateful for _____

_____

_____

_____

I practiced self-care today by_____

_____

_____

_____

_____

_____

_____

_____

_____

_____

_____

♡ ♡ ♡ ♡ Daily Affirmations ♡ ♡ ♡ ♡

I am _____

I am _____

I am _____

Plan Your Work and Work Your Plan!

Set Goal _____

_____

_____

Plan Strategy _____

_____

_____

Outcome _____

_____

_____

Reflect, Release, Recharge & Renew
♡ Positive Self-Talk ONLY ♡
Talk to yourself like you would someone you LOVE. ~ Brené Brown

Update Your Vision Board

Wake up every morning feeling

HAPPY

CONFIDENT

And READY

To CONQUER the Day!

Self-Care is not about self-indulgence,
it's about self-preservation.

~ Audrey Lorde

Self-Care Affirmations

I am grateful to be alive.

I am intentionally eating healthy and exercising daily.

I am the architect of my fate.

C. A. F. E.
Reflections

Connect ■ Ask Questions ■ Find Resources ■ Elevate

It is time to reflect on how far you have come and all that you have learned and accomplished on this self-care journey.

- Take some time to connect with your inner self, ask yourself what you need, find resources to fulfill that need, and elevate to the next level.
- Be open, transparent, and vulnerable with yourself as you explore and evaluate the thoughts and emotions that surface.
- Do not try to hide or conceal any parts of YOU.
- Keep no secrets and tell no lies because that is the only way to grow from your experiences and apply truth to your life.
- Pay close attention to shifts in your attitude, expectations, and goals.

While on this self-care journey, work to become the best version of your authentic self.

 # Reflective Suggestions

- How do you feel at this moment?
- Do you let matters that are out of your control frustrate and overwhelm you?
- Are you achieving the goals you set for yourself?
- What are you holding on to that you need to let go?
- How much time are you giving to people and things that matter most in your life?
- What have you discovered about yourself?
- What changes do you need to make to achieve your personal and professional goals?
- What have you accomplished that makes your heart and soul smile?

The journey into self-love and self-acceptance must begin with self-examination…until you take the journey of self-reflection, it is almost impossible to grow or learn in life.

~ Iyanla Vanzant

C.A.F.E Reflections

Fill your HEART with positive words and symbols that honor who you are and what you love.

Day: _____ Date: _____/_____/_____

Today I am grateful for _____

_____

_____

_____

I practiced self-care today by_____

_____

_____

_____

_____

_____

_____

_____

_____

_____

_____

♡ ♡ ♡ ♡ Daily Affirmations ♡ ♡ ♡ ♡

I am _____

I am _____

I am _____

Plan Your Work and Work Your Plan!

Set Goal _____

_____

_____

Plan Strategy _____

_____

_____

Outcome _____

_____

_____

Day: _____ Date: _____/_____/_____

Today I am grateful for _____
_____
_____
_____

I practiced self-care today by_____
_____
_____
_____
_____
_____
_____
_____
_____
_____
_____
_____

♡ ♡ ♡ ♡ Daily Affirmations ♡ ♡ ♡ ♡

I am _____

I am _____

I am _____

Plan Your Work and Work Your Plan!

Set Goal _____

_____

_____

Plan Strategy _____

_____

_____

Outcome _____

_____

_____

Day: _____ Date: _____/_____/_____

Today I am grateful for _____

_____

_____

_____

I practiced self-care today by_____

_____

_____

_____

_____

_____

_____

_____

_____

_____

_____

♡ ♡ ♡ ♡ Daily Affirmations ♡ ♡ ♡ ♡

I am _____

I am _____

I am _____

Plan Your Work and Work Your Plan!

Set Goal _____

_____

_____

Plan Strategy _____

_____

_____

Outcome _____

_____

_____

Day: _____ Date: _____/_____/_____

Today I am grateful for _____

_____

_____

_____

I practiced self-care today by_____

_____

_____

_____

_____

_____

_____

_____

_____

_____

_____

_____

♡ ♡ ♡ ♡ Daily Affirmations ♡ ♡ ♡ ♡

I am _____

I am _____

I am _____

Plan Your Work and Work Your Plan!

Set Goal _____
_____
_____

Plan Strategy _____
_____
_____

Outcome _____
_____
_____

Day: _____ Date: _____/ _____/ _____

Today I am grateful for _____

_____

_____

_____

I practiced self-care today by_____

_____

_____

_____

_____

_____

_____

_____

_____

_____

_____

_____

♡ ♡ ♡ ♡ Daily Affirmations ♡ ♡ ♡ ♡

I am _____

I am _____

I am _____

Plan Your Work and Work Your Plan!

Set Goal _____

_____

_____

Plan Strategy _____

_____

_____

Outcome _____

_____

_____

Day: _____ Date: _____/ _____/ _____

Today I am grateful for _____
_____
_____
_____

I practiced self-care today by_____
_____
_____
_____
_____
_____
_____
_____
_____
_____
_____
_____

♡ ♡ ♡ ♡ Daily Affirmations ♡ ♡ ♡ ♡

I am _____

I am _____

I am _____

> **Plan Your Work and Work Your Plan!**

Set Goal _____

_____

_____

Plan Strategy _____

_____

_____

Outcome _____

_____

_____

Day: _____ Date: _____ / _____ / _____ ♥

Today I am grateful for _____

_____

_____

_____

I practiced self-care today by _____

_____

_____

_____

_____

_____

_____

_____

_____

_____

_____

♡ ♡ ♡ ♡ Daily Affirmations ♡ ♡ ♡ ♡

I am _____

I am _____

I am _____

Plan Your Work and Work Your Plan!

Set Goal _____

_____

_____

Plan Strategy _____

_____

_____

Outcome _____

_____

_____

Reflect, Release, Recharge & Renew
♡ Positive Self-Talk ONLY ♡
Talk to yourself like you would someone you LOVE. ~ Brené Brown

Every one of us needs to show how much we care for each other and, in the process, care for ourselves.

~ Diana, Princess of Wales

Self-Care Affirmations

I am an example of the kind of world I want to live in.

I am blessed with a supportive family and amazing friends.

I am going to trust the process even when I don't understand it.

Day: _____ Date: _____ / _____ / _____

Today I am grateful for _____

_____

_____

_____

I practiced self-care today by _____

_____

_____

_____

_____

_____

_____

_____

_____

_____

_____

_____

♡ ♡ ♡ ♡ Daily Affirmations ♡ ♡ ♡ ♡

I am _____

I am _____

I am _____

> Plan Your Work and Work Your Plan!

Set Goal _____

_____

_____

Plan Strategy _____

_____

_____

Outcome _____

_____

_____

Day: _____ Date: _____/_____/_____

Today I am grateful for _____

_____

_____

_____

I practiced self-care today by_____

_____

_____

_____

_____

_____

_____

_____

_____

_____

_____

♡ ♡ ♡ ♡ Daily Affirmations ♡ ♡ ♡ ♡

I am _____

I am _____

I am _____

Plan Your Work and Work Your Plan!

Set Goal _____
_____
_____

Plan Strategy _____
_____
_____

Outcome _____
_____
_____

Day: _____ Date: _____/ _____/ _____

Today I am grateful for _____

_____

_____

_____

I practiced self-care today by_____

_____

_____

_____

_____

_____

_____

_____

_____

_____

_____

_____

♡ ♡ ♡ ♡   Daily Affirmations   ♡ ♡ ♡ ♡

I am _____

I am _____

I am _____

> **Plan Your Work and Work Your Plan!**

Set Goal _____

_____

_____

Plan Strategy _____

_____

_____

Outcome _____

_____

_____

Day: _____ Date: _____/ _____/ _____

Today I am grateful for _____

_____

_____

_____

I practiced self-care today by_____

_____

_____

_____

_____

_____

_____

_____

_____

_____

_____

♡ ♡ ♡ ♡ Daily Affirmations ♡ ♡ ♡ ♡

I am _____

I am _____

I am _____

Plan Your Work and Work Your Plan!

Set Goal _____
_____
_____

Plan Strategy _____
_____
_____

Outcome _____
_____
_____

Day: _____ Date: _____/ _____/ _____

Today I am grateful for _____

_____

_____

_____

I practiced self-care today by_____

_____

_____

_____

_____

_____

_____

_____

_____

_____

_____

♡ ♡ ♡ ♡ Daily Affirmations ♡ ♡ ♡ ♡

I am _____

I am _____

I am _____

Plan Your Work and Work Your Plan!

Set Goal _____

_____

_____

Plan Strategy _____

_____

_____

Outcome _____

_____

_____

Day: _____ Date: _____/ _____/ _____

Today I am grateful for _____

_____

_____

_____

I practiced self-care today by_____

_____

_____

_____

_____

_____

_____

_____

_____

_____

_____

♡ ♡ ♡ ♡ Daily Affirmations ♡ ♡ ♡ ♡

I am _____

I am _____

I am _____

Plan Your Work and Work Your Plan!

Set Goal _____

_____

_____

Plan Strategy _____

_____

_____

Outcome _____

_____

_____

Day: _____ Date: _____/_____/_____ ♥

Today I am grateful for _____

_____

_____

_____

I practiced self-care today by_____

_____

_____

_____

_____

_____

_____

_____

_____

_____

_____

♡ ♡ ♡ ♡ Daily Affirmations ♡ ♡ ♡ ♡

I am _____

I am _____

I am _____

Plan Your Work and Work Your Plan!

Set Goal _____
_____
_____

Plan Strategy _____
_____
_____

Outcome _____
_____
_____

Reflect, Release, Recharge & Renew
♡ Positive Self-Talk ONLY ♡
Talk to yourself like you would someone you LOVE. ~ Brené Brown

Self-care is giving the world the best of you instead of what's left of you.

~ Katie Reed

Self-Care Affirmations

I am giving myself permission, time, and space to rest and recharge.

I am at peace with my solitude.

I am giving my burdens to God and find rest in Him.

Day: _____ Date: _____/ _____/ _____

Today I am grateful for _____

_____

_____

_____

I practiced self-care today by_____

_____

_____

_____

_____

_____

_____

_____

_____

_____

♡ ♡ ♡ ♡ Daily Affirmations ♡ ♡ ♡ ♡

I am _____

I am _____

I am _____

Plan Your Work and Work Your Plan!

Set Goal _____
_____
_____

Plan Strategy _____
_____
_____

Outcome _____
_____
_____

Day: _____ Date: _____/_____/_____

Today I am grateful for _____

_____

_____

_____

I practiced self-care today by_____

_____

_____

_____

_____

_____

_____

_____

_____

_____

_____

♡ ♡ ♡ ♡ Daily Affirmations ♡ ♡ ♡ ♡

I am _____

I am _____

I am _____

Plan Your Work and Work Your Plan!

Set Goal _____

_____

_____

Plan Strategy _____

_____

_____

Outcome _____

_____

_____

Day: _____ Date: _____/_____/_____

Today I am grateful for _____

_____

_____

_____

I practiced self-care today by_____

_____

_____

_____

_____

_____

_____

_____

_____

_____

_____

_____

♡ ♡ ♡ ♡ Daily Affirmations ♡ ♡ ♡ ♡

I am _____

I am _____

I am _____

Plan Your Work and Work Your Plan!

Set Goal _____

_____

_____

Plan Strategy _____

_____

_____

Outcome _____

_____

_____

Day: _____ Date: _____/_____/_____

Today I am grateful for _____
_____
_____
_____

I practiced self-care today by_____
_____
_____
_____
_____
_____
_____
_____
_____
_____
_____
_____

♡ ♡ ♡ ♡ Daily Affirmations ♡ ♡ ♡ ♡

I am _____

I am _____

I am _____

Plan Your Work and Work Your Plan!

Set Goal _____

_____

_____

Plan Strategy _____

_____

_____

Outcome _____

_____

_____

Day: _____ Date: _____/ _____/ _____ ♥

Today I am grateful for _____

_____

_____

_____

I practiced self-care today by_____

_____

_____

_____

_____

_____

_____

_____

_____

_____

_____

_____

♡ ♡ ♡ ♡ Daily Affirmations ♡ ♡ ♡ ♡

I am _____

I am _____

I am _____

Plan Your Work and Work Your Plan!

Set Goal _____

_____

_____

Plan Strategy _____

_____

_____

Outcome _____

_____

_____

Day: _____ Date: _____/ _____/ _____

Today I am grateful for _____

_____

_____

_____

I practiced self-care today by_____

_____

_____

_____

_____

_____

_____

_____

_____

_____

_____

_____

♡ ♡ ♡ ♡ Daily Affirmations ♡ ♡ ♡ ♡

I am _____

I am _____

I am _____

Plan Your Work and Work Your Plan!

Set Goal _____

_____

_____

Plan Strategy _____

_____

_____

Outcome _____

_____

_____

Day: _____ Date: _____/ _____/ _____

Today I am grateful for _____

_____

_____

_____

I practiced self-care today by_____

_____

_____

_____

_____

_____

_____

_____

_____

_____

_____

_____

♡ ♡ ♡ ♡ Daily Affirmations ♡ ♡ ♡ ♡

I am _____

I am _____

I am _____

Plan Your Work and Work Your Plan!

Set Goal _____

_____

_____

Plan Strategy _____

_____

_____

Outcome _____

_____

_____

Reflect, Release, Recharge & Renew
♡ Positive Self-Talk ONLY ♡
Talk to yourself like you would someone you LOVE. ~ Brené Brown

Almost anything will work again if you unplug it for a few minutes, including you.

~ Anne Lamott

Self-Care Affirmations

I am taking brain breaks throughout the day.

I am listening to the needs of my body.

I am my best self when I get adequate rest.

Day: _____ Date: _____/ _____/ _____

Today I am grateful for _____

_____

_____

_____

I practiced self-care today by_____

_____

_____

_____

_____

_____

_____

_____

_____

_____

_____

♡ ♡ ♡ ♡ Daily Affirmations ♡ ♡ ♡ ♡

I am _____

I am _____

I am _____

Plan Your Work and Work Your Plan!

Set Goal _____

_____

_____

Plan Strategy _____

_____

_____

Outcome _____

_____

_____

Day: _____ Date: _____/ _____/ _____

Today I am grateful for _____

_____

_____

_____

I practiced self-care today by_____

_____

_____

_____

_____

_____

_____

_____

_____

_____

_____

_____

♡ ♡ ♡ ♡ Daily Affirmations ♡ ♡ ♡ ♡

I am _____

I am _____

I am _____

Plan Your Work and Work Your Plan!

Set Goal _____

_____

_____

Plan Strategy _____

_____

_____

Outcome _____

_____

_____

Day: _____ Date: _____/ _____/ _____

Today I am grateful for _____

_____

_____

_____

I practiced self-care today by_____

_____

_____

_____

_____

_____

_____

_____

_____

_____

_____

♡ ♡ ♡ ♡ Daily Affirmations ♡ ♡ ♡ ♡

I am _____

I am _____

I am _____

Plan Your Work and Work Your Plan!

Set Goal _____

_____

_____

Plan Strategy _____

_____

_____

Outcome _____

_____

_____

Day: _____ Date: _____/_____/_____

Today I am grateful for _____

_____

_____

_____

I practiced self-care today by_____

_____

_____

_____

_____

_____

_____

_____

_____

_____

_____

♡ ♡ ♡ ♡ Daily Affirmations ♡ ♡ ♡ ♡

I am _____

I am _____

I am _____

> Plan Your Work and Work Your Plan!

Set Goal _____
_____
_____

Plan Strategy _____
_____
_____

Outcome _____
_____
_____

Day: _____ Date: _____/_____/_____ ♥

Today I am grateful for _____

_____

_____

_____

I practiced self-care today by_____

_____

_____

_____

_____

_____

_____

_____

_____

_____

_____

_____

♡ ♡ ♡ ♡ Daily Affirmations ♡ ♡ ♡ ♡

I am _____

I am _____

I am _____

Plan Your Work and Work Your Plan!

Set Goal _____

_____

_____

Plan Strategy _____

_____

_____

Outcome _____

_____

_____

Day: _____ Date: _____ / _____ / _____

Today I am grateful for _____

_____

_____

_____

I practiced self-care today by _____

_____

_____

_____

_____

_____

_____

_____

_____

_____

_____

_____

♡ ♡ ♡ ♡ Daily Affirmations ♡ ♡ ♡ ♡

I am _____

I am _____

I am _____

Plan Your Work and Work Your Plan!

Set Goal _____

_____

_____

Plan Strategy _____

_____

_____

Outcome _____

_____

_____

Day: _____ Date: _____/ _____/ _____

Today I am grateful for _____

_____

_____

_____

I practiced self-care today by_____

_____

_____

_____

_____

_____

_____

_____

_____

_____

_____

♡ ♡ ♡ ♡ Daily Affirmations ♡ ♡ ♡ ♡

I am _____

I am _____

I am _____

> Plan Your Work and Work Your Plan!

Set Goal _____

_____

_____

Plan Strategy _____

_____

_____

Outcome _____

_____

_____

Reflect, Release, Recharge & Renew
♡ Positive Self-Talk ONLY ♡
Talk to yourself like you would someone you LOVE. ~ Brené Brown

Update Your Vision Board

The stories you tell yourself everyday will either

LIFT you up

Or

TEAR you down.

Monitor your thought life and speak truth over yourself.

C. A. F. E.
Reflections

Connect ▪ Ask Questions ▪ Find Resources ▪ Elevate

It is time to reflect on how far you have come and all that you have learned and accomplished on this self-care journey.

- Take some time to connect with your inner self, ask yourself what you need, find resources to fulfill that need, and elevate to the next level.
- Be open, transparent, and vulnerable with yourself as you explore and evaluate the thoughts and emotions that surface.
- Do not try to hide or conceal any parts of YOU.
- Keep no secrets and tell no lies because that is the only way to grow from your experiences and apply truth to your life.
- Pay close attention to shifts in your attitude, expectations, and goals.

While on this self-care journey, work to become the best version of your authentic self.

♡♡♡ Reflective Suggestions ♡♡♡

- How do you feel at this moment?

- Do you let matters that are out of your control frustrate and overwhelm you?

- Are you achieving the goals you set for yourself?

- What are you holding on to that you need to let go?

- How much time are you giving to people and things that matter most in your life?

- What have you discovered about yourself?

- What changes do you need to make to achieve your personal and professional goals?

- What have you accomplished that makes your heart and soul smile?

Without reflection, we go blindly on our way creating more unintended consequences and failing to achieve anything useful.

~ Margaret J. Wheatley

C.A.F.E Reflections

I am

learning

growing

thriving

and **BECOMING**

a better version of myself

every day!

Keep It Going

Whether you are an avid self-care enthusiast or just now committing to taking the first steps on this journey, keep going. The goal is to become a little healthier and happier every day. Share your progress and inspire your friends and family to do the same.

Maintain a growth mindset so that you will continue to be a life-long learner. Self-care is a life-long commitment to being the absolute best YOU! Take the information and tips that you learned along the way and apply them to every aspect of your life. Commit to being just a tad bit better each day. Remember, small, consistent changes and time yield BIG results.

Though some days can be a struggle, it's important to have something that will motivate, inspire, and help us stay positive and keep moving forward.

~ Demi Levato

My Commitment

Make a commitment to yourself on how you will continue your self-care journey. It might mean starting a new journal, nurturing that garden you planted or learning a new skill. You choose what works for you. Whatever you do, do not stop learning and growing. You have come too far to turn back now. As previously discussed, writing down your goals and sharing them with someone will make them more achievable.

_____

_____

_____

_____

_____

_____

_____

_____

_____

_____

Self-Care Pledge

I, _____, promise to make self-care a top priority. I pledge to cultivate habits that honor ME, reduce stress, and enhance my overall health and well-being. I will take time each day to invest in ME, mind, body, and soul because I am worth it. My needs matter too!

Signed _____

Let's Stay Connected

I am so honored that you joined me on this self-care journey to better health and wellness. I hope this journal has been helpful, and you are stronger, healthier, and happier.

While you are here, please take a minute to follow me on Facebook, Instagram, and YouTube for self-care tips, tools, strategies, and challenges. Connect with me on LinkedIn too. I would love to hear how you utilized the journal and where you are on your self-care journey.

Join the Facebook Saving Ourselves Support Group (facebook.com/groups/154955292586988) to stay inspired and to inspire others.

You can find self-care products and resources, including my blog and books, at drgwenscounselorcafe.com

   @drgwenscounselorcafe

   @drgwenscounselorcafe

    linkedin.com/in/drgwenscafe/

   Dr. Gwen's Counselor Cafe

Self-Care Domain Activities

Physical self-care involves activities that help you stay fit and healthy.

Physical Self-Care

- Eat healthy
- Exercise regularly
- Get regular check-ups
- Hot bath
- Massage
- Sexual needs
- Sleep (7-8 hours)
- Stay hydrated
- Take power naps
- Wear clothes that make you feel good
- Yoga

Psychological self-care involves engaging in activities that improve your mental strength, engage your intellect, stimulate you, and keep your mind sharp.

Psychological Self-Care

- Engage in hobbies
- Go to museums
- Keep a reflection journal
- Learn a new skill
- Listen to a podcast
- Receive compliments
- Say NO without feeling guilty
- Social time with family and friends

Emotional self-care is allowing yourself to safely experience and navigate your full range of emotions.

Emotional Self-Care

- Compliment (yourself)
- Feel your feelings (cry, laugh)
- Forgive
- Join a group (social, support)
- Keep a mood journal
- Read books
- Show kindness and compassion
- Spend time with loved ones
- Talk to someone you trust (coach, counselor mentor)
- Watch movies

Spiritual self-care involves beliefs, values, perspective, and purpose beyond day-to-day life that are important to you.

Spiritual Self-Care

- Attend a worship service
- Daily devotion
- Donate (money, resources, time)
- Inspirational (books, groups, podcast, videos)
- Meditate/Pray
- Spend time alone
- Spend time in nature
- Write in a gratitude journal

Professional self-care involves work/life balance and understanding your purpose in your role.

Professional Self-Care

- Arrive and leave on time
- Brain breaks
- Daily lunch break
- Echo chamber
- Form collaborative relationships
- Happy journal (positive things that happen at work).
- Learn to say no
- Professional development
- Seek challenges
- Set boundaries
- Take a course or attend a conference/workshop
- Use vacation time and sick days
- Work with a mentor

Acknowledgements

THANK YOU to my husband, Carl. Your sacrifice and support allowed me the time and space to create this journal. Without your unconditional love, I would not be able to pursue my life's passion.

My rich cultural upbringing taught me the importance of family and community. Thanks, mom, and dad, for providing those experiences that have become a big part of who I am and what I do.

I have a phenomenal extended family that showers me with love, support, and encouragement. Ms. Betty Jo, Sherilyn, and Janice, thanks for everything. You make this small-town girl believe she can do anything.

In my professional life, I have met some amazing people who in most cases I now call friends. My circle of support is full of strong, intelligent, compassionate, helpful, individuals who inspire me. I have learned so much from so many people over the course of my career. I am standing on the shoulders of all of you who paved the way for me.

Thank you to my group members (Saving Ourselves Self-Care Group) for motivating me to keep learning, growing, and creating self-care content and materials.

Finally, thank you to my publishing coach, Lorna Lewis. I appreciate your guidance and support.

♡ ~ Notes ~ ♡

 ~ Notes ~

♡ ~ Notes ~ ♡

 ~ Notes ~

 ~ Notes ~

♡ ~ Notes ~ ♡

Dr. Gwen's Counselor Cafe

Additional Self-Care Products

drgwenscounselorcafe.com/shop

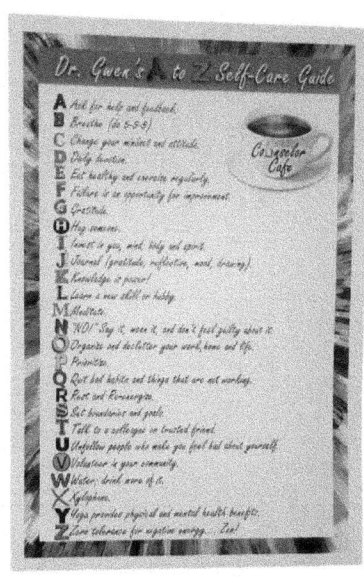

Meet Dr. Gwen

Gwendolyn Martin, who goes by the name Dr. Gwen is a licensed professional counselor, educator (special education teacher, school counselor, professor), and advocate who is dedicated to spotlighting the importance of self-care in managing stress and cultivating health and happiness. She is the owner of Dr. Gwen's Counselor Café, a platform that provides effective self-care solutions for educators, including teachers, counselors, licensed clinicians, and other helping professionals. Her self-care products, group, workshops, speaking engagements, mentoring, consultation, and books help people transform their personal and professional lives. When she isn't working, she invests in self-care by spending time with her loved ones, nurturing her garden, cooking healthy vegetarian/pescatarian dishes, and cuddling up with a good romance novel. You can find out more about Dr. Gwen at drgwenscounselorcafe.com.

www.ingramcontent.com/pod-product-compliance
Lightning Source LLC
LaVergne TN
LVHW061217060426
835508LV00014B/1339